BRAHMINS & BULLYBOYS

Young debutante Miss Rose Fitzgerald (*right*) and her mother, Mrs. John F. Fitzgerald. Boston, 1911

BRAHMINS & BULLYBOYS

G. Frank Radway's Boston Album

Photographs collected with
an introduction and a narrative by
Stephen Halpert & Brenda Halpert

HOUGHTON MIFFLIN COMPANY BOSTON   1973

First Printing   w

Printed in the United States of America

Library of Congress Cataloging in Publication Data

Radway, G   Frank, 1886-1938.
  Brahmins & bullyboys.

  Bibliography: p.
  1. Boston—Social life and customs—Pictorial works.
2. Boston—Social life and customs. I. Halpert,
Stephen. II. Halpert, Brenda.   III. Title.
F73.5.R16   917.44′61′00222   73-177535
ISBN 0-395-17217-9

Portions of this book have appeared in
slightly different form in *American Heritage*.

TO RUTH & ANITA

And the memories of Robin & Travis

Contents

Portrait of the artist. G. Frank Radway, circa 1920

Elegy for a
News Photographer

PHOTOGRAPHS HAVE A WAY of unlocking history. By reaching back into our heritage, they add vitality and lyrical insight to the ofttimes cold and impersonal observations of the trained historian. An early photograph can lend spontaneity to an otherwise forgotten moment, placing the past within the immediate grasp and understanding of the present. Working with little social bias and following his daily assignment sheet, the early news photographer was always searching out the unusual, his simple box camera recording the very essence of truth — truth too immediate and particular to be readily grasped by conventional historians.

This book presents a collection of socially and historically relevant photographs of Boston and vicinity, taken between 1890 and 1920 by G. Frank Radway, a highly perceptive, if unknown, photographer. During his youth and for almost thirty years as a staff photographer for the Boston *Advertiser* (later the Boston *Record American*), Radway contributed to our cultural development and our history by capturing our unchartered and forgotten moments in time — the very life experience, the humor, and the pathos or emotion of another age. As individual works of art and as social commentary, his photographs reflect much of the fashion and decorum of the first quarter of this century. The fact that life was extremely difficult and cruel in those days (unless one was fortunate enough to have been born into Brahmin wealth and privilege) was one such reality innocently captured by Radway's lens. Through his work, one can witness a slice of life not frequently discussed in other chronicles and personal reminiscences about life in Boston — a city often referred to in such books as ''the Athens of America.''

It is certainly true that Boston has always

been a city of great wealth and learning, a city proud of its Anglican tradition. However, to call the city "the Athens of America" is to exaggerate the facts. In Boston's history, poverty, slums, religious discrimination, and unemployment have been as much a part of life as the wealth and culture of the lofty Brahmins. Most of the important writers, chroniclers, and historians of Boston were heirs of that blue blood; they therefore paid little attention to Irish immigrants, considering Irish activities of very little consequence. As a result Boston was — and still is — depicted as a city where poverty is nonexistent or at most minimal. However, the truth is that poverty was not only influential in determining the style and attitude of ordinary Bostonians but also a deciding factor in any analysis of the city's economic and political pathos. Though the Irish failed to gain control of Boston's actual wealth, they succeeded rather well in determining how a portion of that wealth could be utilized — by taking over the political reins of the city. Ultimately, the Brahmins and the Irish accepted each other, each group recognizing that the other was a force with which to be reckoned. At times, the two groups even cooperated with each other. But it was cooperation born of expediency, not mutual desire.

The men who made the first forays into the political arena — John "Honey" Fitzgerald and his successor, James Michael Curley — were outspoken defiers of decorum and the status quo. They were tough political bosses, adept in the use of power and capable of generating and receiving great love. Through these men, the Irish became recognized; perhaps the Brahmins never learned to understand the Irish temperament, but they acknowledged its force.

Like most city dwellers of seventy years ago — in an age when political bosses were strong and articulate — Bostonians were susceptible to the style and theatrics of colorful spokesmen. Today, it is difficult to understand the dimensions of these men who were so charismatic when speaking to crowds. Their voices and their histories are largely forgotten, in the way that yesterday's headlines drift into obscurity. But in photographs one can see some of their qualities, and it is these qualities that Radway captured in his daily newspaper assignments.

As a newspaper photographer, Radway had to cover a variety of scenes: a fire in Salem, the imprisonment of a union leader, the proud and defiant faces of the political majority on the one hand, the blushing bride on the other. In this work, was Radway simply an echo to his times, or was he what Camus might have considered a true witness to man's comic pose? Little is known of Radway's personal life. His ambition was limited; his responsibility and loyalty were seemingly directed toward his newspaper, the Boston *Advertiser* (later the *Record American*), to whose service he gave over half of his life. Born in Swampscott, Massachusetts, on June 30, 1886, "Rad," as he was later called, lived for a number of years in Utica, New York. Upon returning to Boston, he joined the photographic staff of the Boston newspaper, where he remained until his death. Referred to as the "most punctual cameraman in the newspaper business," he was late for work only once during his entire career — seven minutes late, to be exact — and was downcast for days as a result. For twenty-nine consecutive years he made pictures of the annual May Day hoop-rolling by Wellesley College seniors, and by the end of his career he had boarded more incoming and outgoing ocean liners than any other newspaperman in the United States. On Wednesday, the seventeenth of August 1938, he died in his home at 31 Falmouth Street in Boston's Back Bay, and was survived by his widow, Mrs. Helene M. Radway.

It is reasonably certain that G. Frank Radway was never singled out and recognized for his unique talent for capturing on film the exact expression and sentiment of his subject. Unlike most artists, he made no attempt to express himself through his subjects; he did not stretch what he saw, or retouch the truth. Probably his only concern was getting his assignments completed and turned in, and he was doubtless unaware of his own extraordinary ability to capture the essence, the truth, of the moment. Radway's talents were never extolled by his peers, nor did he seek special praise. He kept his place, followed orders well, and — fortunately for posterity — took pictures through which we can now relive history.

Radway unwittingly witnessed and recorded the gradual development of Boston from a prosaic nineteenth-century town to a city of international finance and power. He watched the final filling in of Boston's Back Bay, the day-to-day political struggles of Honey Fitz, James Michael Curley, James Jackson Storrow, and Leverett Saltonstall. He laughed at such passing fancies as a swim in the Charles River and the driving of an early automobile up the State House steps. The Radway lens captured the faces and attitudes long obscured by more poignant and persistent memories.

The faces in the crowd . . . some unknown, some forgotten, some remembered. One face in the Boston crowd was the young Joseph P. Kennedy, just beginning to join the celebrity parade but still unknown to the point of being identified in one photograph only as "Kennedy." Then he was even less a public figure than Miss Rose Fitzgerald, daughter of Mayor John ("Honey Fitz") Fitzgerald, whose debut guest list provides a subtle hint of her future with a man named Kennedy and what that marriage would mean to Boston and to the United States more than four decades later.

Radway's camera saw Albert Einstein, his hair flying in all directions, on a visit to Boston; and Claude Grahame-White, when he was making history with biplane flights from the Harvard Aviation Field — long before East Bostonians opposed the use of supersonic jet planes at Logan Airport. Roosevelt, Taft, Harding — all visited Boston, each making his way through the disorganized streets of the city in an open touring car. And Calvin Coolidge, another White House occupant, gained national prominence with his handling of the 1919 Boston police strike.

The camera could not tell us — we who are privy to the news of half a century between then and now—that Governor Coolidge's young son, with him during his gubernatorial inauguration, would die before reaching maturity; or that Joseph and Rose would become parents of a President, a U.S. attorney general, and three U.S. senators. It would be the sons of the casually identified Joseph Kennedy and the demure debutante Rose who would break America's religious barriers for the presidency, and who would inherit, with their Harvard accent, a new Brahmin domain in the Bullyboy world of politics.

In a similar way, Cardinal O'Connell was unaware of changes to come. Unchallenged as yet in his own realm, he could not foresee that the Church would one day feel the relentless pressure of ecumenicalism and the new Mass, of Third World priests, of Daniel and Philip Berrigan.

Spindle-legged Babe Ruth is pictured by

Radway's camera in a rare unsmiling mood. Ruth, who would become the Sultan of Swat, was sold to New York and was lost to Boston sports fans for most of his career. However, he was to return in the thirties, with his boyish grin, on an older pair of skinnier legs and with a fatter belly behind a fading but still beautiful swing. This was an age of war, new uniforms, puttees, Sam Browne belts, and columns marching through Park Square. Samuel Gompers fought battles for organized labor, and derby-hatted throngs filled the streets of Boston to shake their fists at "the bosses."

It was the beginning of the end for many things and people, the eclipse of others. The Indians are photographed merely as a curiosity, in native costumes and headdresses, their faces affluent with the sadness of poverty. The black man is almost nowhere to be found, still lost in the city ghetto; unchained perhaps, but imprisoned by a wall of segregation higher than the Customs House. His fight for freedom would come later, when an electronic form of communication called television would bring into the homes of all Americans the civil rights confrontations of the sixties and seventies.

Long before the rhetoric of liberation was first heard at Ford Hall Forum, suffragettes were beginning to dispute male dominance, questioning their half citizenship and demanding the right to vote. For the female stars of the theater (and an emerging Hollywood) only the clothes were different. The instant smile, the frozen pose — the aura of glamour and mystery was there, especially for those who looked for it.

As always some Bostonians found time to engage in crime. The automobile was beginning to fill a new page in the diary of accidents and casualties. Boston society was selfish of its Brahmin past and turned up its nose to the Radway lens in a gesture that required no caption. Bathing suits were beginning to show knees as well as ankles; Buffalo Bill's Wild West Show came to town; the city of Salem almost burned down. There were gypsy dancers on the Fenway, food handouts for the poor at Christmas, promenading throngs at Revere Beach in summer, historical restorations, and new electric trolley cars.

Any day could bring you a picture of John L. Sullivan, J. Pierpont Morgan, Jr., Henry Ford, Dr. Edward Everett Hale, Sir Harry Lauder, Sir Thomas Lipton, Dr. Charles P. Steinmetz, Helen Keller, Queen Elizabeth of Belgium, and so many others who came to Boston to see and be seen. All of them were captured by Radway's lens so that we, decades later, could see them too, in our own way and in our own time.

STEPHEN HALPERT
BRENDA HALPERT

BRAHMINS & BULLYBOYS

Radway's World

BOSTON AT THE MIDDLE of the nineteenth century...

James Knox Polk was President in Washington and George N. Briggs was governor of Massachusetts, when Dr. J. V. C. Smith, candidate for mayor of Boston, announced that South Boston was sure to become "the magnificent portion of the city, with costly residences, fashionable society, and the influence of wealth."

He was wrong. Union Park was laid out in 1851 as the social center of the city, but people clung to the West End and Beacon Hill. The Back Bay was a large picturesque marsh, bounded on the east by the Public Garden. Beacon Street ran straight westward through the marsh, and flocks of wild ducks were frightened by early morning tradesmen and their wagons on the mill dam.

A rapidly growing city in 1850, Boston had not entirely lost the Puritan heritage of her earlier days, when she had been just a colonial village and her women forbidden by law to wear short sleeves, "whereby the nakedness of the arm may be disclosed," or "silke or tiffany hoods," unless the wearer had a "visible estate" of two hundred pounds.

Nor had she lost her stature as a major port city — a position earned in the eighteenth century by several generations of thrifty, ambitious, and courageous Yankees. But Boston would not become, in the nineteenth century, the greatest American city. Although Boston society was much older than New York's, and its wealth per capita much greater, the tide had turned to New York City, through a combination of geographical, political, and historical circumstances.

Nonetheless, Boston continued to prosper commercially for many decades. The Yankee strain still produced men of strong character and shrewd business sense. Boston became the leader in wool, leather, footwear, seafood, and coffee roasting and grinding. It was largely Boston money that established the railroads of America; it was Boston ingenuity that opened the first copper mines in the Lake Superior regions; and it was Boston men who taught New York and growing western cities nearly all they knew of banking, finance, and huge industrial combinations. The names Peabody, Morgan, Higginson, Lee, Morrow, Dawes, and Young come to mind — not all of them were Boston-born, but all were of the old Massachusetts Colony stock that has always led industry in this country; and most of them were prominently identified with Boston at some point in their careers.

As a residential city, as a center of education, music, and the fine arts, nineteenth-century Boston exemplified the best the nation had to offer. Only a sense of humor was lacking. The Boston ideal of cordial hospitality, during these times, seems to have invited the stranger within the gates to occupy a place in the family pew at church. "I am afraid to say," wrote Dickens, "how many offers of pews and seats in church were made to us by formal invitation that morning of my arrival (which was on Sunday) . . . but at least as many sittings as would have accommodated a score or two of grown up families!"

One of the few acceptable activities outside the home or the church during the mid-nineteenth century was attendance at "the club"— for men, that is. In 1848 there was only "one" club for men in Boston — the Temple. It preserved the stately traditions of White's and Brooks' clubs in London. Example: no member took off his hat in the clubrooms, a custom borrowed from the House of Commons.

The Somerset Club was an offspring of the Temple, and was founded in 1852 as the Tremont Club. Later, when it moved to Somerset Street, it took its present name. The Union Club, as its name implies, was originally a patriotic organization formed during the Civil War. Later in the century, dining clubs became popular, as did some social, literary, and even politically oriented groups. The Wednesday Evening Club had been in continuous existence since 1776. There were no clubs for women, however, until 1868, when the New England Women's Club was established, though not as a place for pleasure or recreation in the sense of a modern club. It was specifically laid down at the outset that this club "was to be no lounging place for the drones." On the contrary, its aim was "to provide opportunity for culture in dignified and deliberate discussion in which they [women] are so lamentably deficient." The club further pointed out that it was "no excrescence but a natural outgrowth of a robust earnest age."

Women's place during the nineteenth century was definitely in the home and Boston ladies, with very few exceptions, led quiet, cloistered lives. It is remarked by many an English visitor that Boston had everything necessary for the most agreeable society, except the spirit of sociability.

The term "New England Brahmin" was created by Oliver Wendell Holmes. In many ways he was a perfect example of the class, and the tastes, prejudices, and follies of the Brahmins are clearly reflected in his writings. The Brahmins were the elite of nineteenth-century Boston, "with their houses by Bulfinch, their monopoly of Beacon Street, their ancestral portraits and Chinese porcelain, humanitarianism,

Unitarian faith in the march of mind, Yankee shrewdness and New England exclusiveness.'' This elite reigned supreme during most of Holmes's life. It was only toward the end of his days that old Boston really began to alter dramatically, its population multiplying rapidly as scores of immigrants poured in. By 1894, the Irish had taken over Boston's political machinery.

To the warm, outgoing Irish, Anglo-Saxon reserve seemed unnatural and unfeeling, and they compared the Yankee to the cold-blooded Atlantic codfish. Holmes did not consider the needs or feelings of the emerging Bullyboy. Though the influx of immigrants had created new social problems, many of which pertained to the Bullyboys, these matters did not find their way into Holmes's writings. He did not participate in the growing trend toward realism in literature and journalism. As a matter of fact, he firmly believed that extreme realism was totally outside the function of literature. Reflecting solid Brahmin tradition, he wrote in *Over the Teacups*: ''A man's vocabulary is terribly retentive of evil words, and the images they present cling to his memory and will not lose their hold. One who has had the mischance to soil his mind reading certain poems of Swift will never cleanse it to its original wholeness.''

Holmes described a New Englander as a person ''of almost pure and unmixed English blood; he is a proud squire, unmellowed, exacerbated and aestheticized by change of climate; for juicy mutton, split cod fish, for the delicate and soothing air of the Gulf Stream, the icy winds of Labrador, for the sweet Hawthorne hedge, the boulder fence . . . [he] is simply an Americanized Englishman. As the Englishman is the physical bully of the world, so the Boston-ian is the aesthetic and intellectual bully of America.''

Naturally, the Brahmins were careful about who could join their select social circles. ''What do I mean by a man of family?'' asked the Autocrat at the first of his celebrated breakfast talks. ''Oh, I'll give you a general idea of what I mean . . . four or five generations of gentlemen and gentle women, among them a member of His Majesty's Council for the Province, a governor or so, one or two Doctors of Divinity, a member of congress not later than the time of long boots and tassels.''

As the old Boston ditty goes:

> *And this is good old Boston,*
> *The Home of the bean and the cod,*
> *Where the Lowells talk to the Cabots*
> *And the Cabots talk only to God.*

While the Brahmins enjoyed the comforts of midcentury Boston, the city itself began to undergo a period of transition and growth. No longer was it an isolated New England seaport, connected to the rest of the nation by ships and bad roads. With its population and industry becoming ever more diversified, Boston would have to expand, and the answer to this need was ''land making'' and annexation.

The city began to fill in the marshes surrounding the thin strip of land that joined the pear-shaped peninsula of Boston to the highlands. The filling in of the land between Boston and Roxbury began, and Roxbury, formerly a separate city with long-standing disagreements with Boston over boundaries, was annexed to Boston. Gravel was brought in and dumped into the stagnant waters, and out of the effort came a new district, the South End. For a brief moment in time, the South End had its day of high fashion. The architecture of the area consisted largely of imposing bow-front town houses, rather more formal than the houses of Beacon Hill. There were, in addition, several large hotels, which were then coming into vogue, offering suites that provided family privacy.

Perhaps the most important single accomplishment in the South End in this period was the completion of the Boston City Hospital in 1858. Of modern design, for those days, the hospital consisted of a central building with a striking dome, used for administration offices, and flanked on each side by a long pavilion for medical and surgical treatment. Auxiliary buildings in the rear housed wards, autopsy rooms, and the morgue.

After the South End, city planners looked toward their final, and perhaps their greatest, achievement — the filling-in of the marshland just south of Beacon Street, the Back Bay. Arthur Gilman was assigned the task of planning the area. He drew up blueprints that called for rectangular blocks, unlike the winding roads of Beacon Hill. Inspired by the boulevards of Paris, Gilman planned his main thoroughfare as a mall flanked by two dual carriageways, leading from the gardens to the outlying areas. The cross streets, paralleling the Public Garden, were given English names in alphabetical order. Lots were then sold at public auction, with profits, approximately four million dollars, going to the state.

Back Bay became *the* residential area of Boston. Its bay-windowed town houses epitomized the peculiar blend of confidence, affluence, and refinement that characterized Boston's elite society. At the same time, the Back Bay became the mecca for all intellectual activity within the city, as a number of colleges and other institu-

tions of higher learning were founded there during the 1850s and 1860s. By 1870, the Back Bay had almost completely usurped the role of the South End as the seat of all that was fashionable and intellectual in Boston. The South End, meanwhile, was left to the greatly expanding and culturally diversified middle class, the Bullyboys.

Although intellectual life flourished in New England, it was not until the 1850s that Bostonians felt the full force of social and political issues that were rocking other areas of the nation. It was easy enough for the Brahmin mind to stand aloof from the issue of slavery. This stance was modified, however, under the pressure of strong advocates of abolition such as William Lloyd Garrison and the Unitarian minister William Ellery Channing. It is not surprising that women — themselves lacking power and autonomy in a man's world — were especially responsive to abolitionist rhetoric. The growing interest in abolition coincided with another intellectual upheaval — the rise of Unitarianism. Which came first — abolitionism or Unitarianism — is difficult to determine, but their advents were definitely related. The liberal spirit they shared, and the strident voices of the abolitionists, stirred protests from more conservative church denominations and others of a conservative turn of mind. No less a man than Nathan Lord, president of Dartmouth College, sent two letters to Boston in which he maintained that slavery was a divine institution according to natural and revealed religion. The general atmosphere in Boston, however, was abolitionist.

Intellectual life in Boston during the fifties and sixties was liberal in philosophy, and literary in tone. In 1853, the Saturday Club was formed in order to bring together the leading writers and thinkers in the area. Members met at the Parker House on the last Saturday of every month to discuss cultural and political matters, and to enjoy a seven-course dinner in a private dining room. Eventually, its members became the major contributors to the newly formed *Atlantic Monthly*. Through this journal the views of the Saturday Club could be spread to a large and appreciative body of readers. Early issues included the philosophy of Emerson, the poetry of Henry Wadsworth Longfellow, James Russell Lowell, John Greenleaf Whittier, William Cullen Bryant, and Oliver Wendell Holmes, the science of Louis Agassiz, and the fiction of Nathaniel Hawthorne. While the *Atlantic Monthly* called for abolition, it was still common for the privileged men of Boston, if they wished, to pay for "stand-ins" to take their places in the Union ranks. Thus it was the poor workingmen who were forced into the ranks of the military. During the summer of 1863, Boston failed to fulfill its requisition for men by voluntary enlistment, and it became necessary to resort to conscription. This effrontery resulted in the Draft Riots of 1863, which were echoed by a greater and more historic riot in New York.

As two marshals were handing out notices to men in the North End, telling them of their conscriptions, they were attacked by irate wives. Local police who came to restore order were beaten and forced to return to their stationhouses. By evening the women had been replaced by their husbands returning from work. These workingclass citizens dared to oppose the government's right to drag them from their homes to fight for a cause in which they did not believe.

Normally quiet townspeople became incensed

rioters by nightfall, and a group of them looted several gun shops in Dock Square. Police blocked all approaches to the square and the rioters were easily contained. The new conscripts went without further trouble, and disturbances in other parts of the city kept the militia on alert for only twenty-four hours.

After the Civil War, Boston entered a more tranquil period, one that allowed time for activity in architecture and other arts. Much of the architectural enterprise was focused around Copley Square, which thereby became one of the finest squares in the country. H. H. Richardson led the way in 1871, with his Romanesque design for what is now the First Baptist Church, just off Copley Square on the corner of Commonwealth Avenue and Clarendon Street. A frieze by Frédéric Auguste Bartholdi adorned the tower; trumpeting angels were placed at the four corners of the frieze, thus winning for the church the nickname "Church of the Holy Beanblowers."

In 1872, the first structure of the Museum of Fine Arts was built in Copley Square. The design was heavily influenced by John Ruskin, outspoken English critic of Renaissance styles of architecture. In 1880, the Commonwealth granted land to the Boston Public Library for a new building in the square. After some delay McKim, Mead, and White were engaged to plan the construction of the building. The exterior was inspired by Henri Labrouste's Library of Sainte Geneviève, while the interior featured murals, frescoes, and sculpture by some of the world's leading artists. Across the street from this magnificent building, at the corner of Boylston and Dartmouth streets, the new Old South Church was built. Designed by Cummings and Sears, the church was notable for its leaning tower, 246 feet high, which continued to lean until it was more than thirty-six inches out of line. It was taken down in 1931, and rebuilt in 1940.

Possibly the finest adornment of Copley Square was Richardson's Trinity Church, located at the east end of the square. With the help of Charles Follen McKim and Stanford White, work was begun in 1874 and completed in 1877. Twenty years later, the porch and triple entrances were to be added by Shepley, Rutan, and Coolidge. Built in the French Romansque style of the eleventh century, including cloisters and a chapel, the church was Richardson's masterpiece. It was raised on 4500 wooden piles that had to be kept moist to prevent them from rotting. At first this was accomplished by a small boat kept beneath the church: when the boat touched bottom, more water was pumped into the area. Today, the water level is automatically controlled, and the massive stone structure weighing nearly nineteen million pounds is still supported on the wooden piles.

Boston advanced in other arts as well. No single artistic endeavor is more characteristic of the Boston Brahmins' interest in culture than the Boston Symphony Orchestra, founded by Henry Lee Higginson in 1881. It was the success of the year, and within a decade was world famous. By 1900, the BSO had established itself as the cornerstone of Boston culture — a position that it has held without interruption to this day.

In literature, too, developments were occurring that would gradually take Boston literary tastes beyond the genteel world of Holmes's works into areas of social conflict. The leader in this movement was William Dean Howells, whose novel *The Rise of Silas Lapham* appeared in 1885 and became one of the most controversial novels of its time. Howells was a very proper Bostonian; born in Martin's Ferry, Ohio, he became more proper than the native Bostonians themselves. In his writings, however, he grappled with social issues of real substance. He did not write much about the issue of the Civil War or the lives of black people, and he did not see far into workingmen's lives. He did, however, begin a trend toward realism in fiction that would culminate in the works of later writers. In *The Rise of Silas Lapham* he depicted the conflicts and differences between the established elite of Boston and the newly rich Lapham family. It is only Penelope, Lapham's literary daughter, who is accepted into the highest circle by marriage. Her acceptance is representative of the first successful incursions by outsiders into the realm of Boston society. In later years, the challenges to Brahmins from the growing numbers of heterogeneous groups would increase. These were the years in which outsiders—the Irish, the Bullyboys—were becoming rich enough and powerful enough to challenge the Brahmin hegemony.

In 1890 Bostonians could look back over forty years of continuous growth. The city had pretty well completed its task of land-filling and expansion. Population grew at a considerable rate: between 1870 and 1890, the number of Boston's inhabitants had risen from 250,000 to 420,000. Although she was no match, in sheer size, with New York or Chicago, Boston was definitely a great metropolis.

The scene was grand and varied near the turn of the century, when Frank Radway started his career with the Boston *Advertiser*. A visitor touring the city could observe many contrasting scenes. If architecturally minded, he could walk from the State House, over Beacon Hill, along Beacon Street, and find along the way nearly every style of architecture employed in Boston in the previous eighty or ninety years. Or, if he chose, he could go over to Washington Street to visit the scene of the Great Fire that swept through downtown Boston on November 9, 1872. A walk along Charles Street would reveal a street that was narrower and cozier than it is today. Shops on that street were largely confined to the blocks between Beacon and Mount Vernon streets, and there were only a few: Clough & Shackley, pharmacist; De Luca's fruit store; and a few others. At Chater's Bakery, our walker could buy a bowl of soup or a ham sandwich for five cents, a chicken sandwich for ten cents.

For out-of-towners, the Parker House, the Hotel Lenox, and the Hotel Vendome were the most fashionable and reasonable places to stay. The Parker House, first Boston hotel to adopt the European plan of accommodations, charged $1.50 and up for a room, excluding meals. The Lenox, too, adopted this plan, but the Vendome continued to charge $5 and up on the American plan.

To the visiting playgoer — or indeed to the resident — Boston afforded a variety of theatrical experiences. During the week of January 20, 1890, Edwin Booth made his final appearance on stage, with his costars Helena Modjeska and Otis Skinner, in *Hamlet, Macbeth,* and *The Fool's Revenge.* During the 1890s, James O'Neill, Eugene's father, appeared in *Monte Cristo* and Eleanora Duse played in *Camille.* In March 1891, a New York theater family presented the Actors' Fund Benefit which introduced George M. Cohen to Boston audiences. The most elegant and respectable theater in town was the Boston Theatre, which faced Washington Street near West Street. By traveling a long passageway at the Washington Street entrance, theatergoers could reach the 3000-seat auditorium. But the person in search of entertainment was not limited to this legitimate theater: he could, if he wished, visit the theaters of Benjamin Franklin Keith, who in 1885 had introduced continuous performances, and thus had begun the vigorous tradition of vaudeville in America.

Despite its worldly pleasures, Boston was more than ever a city of churches. The Back Bay, as we have seen, had many notable Protestant churches, while Roman Catholics — by now a majority — had raised numerous buildings around town. Boston continued to be the breeding ground of new sects in the late nineteenth century: in 1879 it became the home of Mary Baker Eddy's Christian Science. This movement was to gain nationwide popularity following the publication in 1875 of her book *Science and Health,* but Boston remained the home of Christian Science, with the mother church and the central economic power of the church based there.

Whatever sobering influences the churches provided were often lost in the whirlwind of the most controversial issue of the Gay Nineties — the question of the Boston saloon, or groggery. During the gubernatorial election of 1890, former Governor John Quincy Adams Brackett ran again as the dry candidate. He had passed a bill appointing police commissioners to regulate Boston's drinking habits. The police board screened every city bar to make sure that patrons drank at tables and not at a counter bar, and patrons were obliged to order food with their drinks. Saloons resorted to the free-lunch ploy, and drinkers aware of the law willingly turned down the dried and moldy sandwiches left as tokens on the tables. Voters preferred the incumbent Democrat, Governor William Eustis Russell, but even he failed to repeal the the law. Most Bostonians continued to drink, law or no law.

As the century drew to a close, Boston was definitely a bustling city. The transport scene gave evidence of this: the Boston transit companies crisscrossed trolley lines on, under, and above city streets; bicycles were all the rage, and horseless carriages were beginning to frighten pedestrians on Commonwealth Avenue. It was a time of confidence and vigor.

Boston welcomed 1900 and the new century with the slogan "A Bigger, Better, Busier Boston." The Boston *Herald* claimed, "If one could not have made money this past year, his case is hopeless." Taxes were minimal, trade was brisk, and prosperity was in the air.

In the new century, the cultural and ethnic diversity of Boston was becoming more marked. The prevailing tone was still that of the traditional Yankees — proud, frugal, well educated, and energetic. These were the people for whom Sarah Bernhardt, in 1901, played with Coquelin Aîné in *Cyrano de Bergerac*. These were the readers of the Boston *Evening Transcript*, which every Wednesday evening carried a column of complete genealogies of Boston First Families. For these people, too, Herbert W. Gleason prepared a monumental new edition of Henry David Thoreau's complete works in 1906. Gleason, a minister turned photographer, recorded Thoreau's favorite haunts on five-by-seven-inch glass plates. These illustrations, as well as careful editing, made Gleason's edition the most attractive and reliable collection of Thoreau's works for many years.

Over and against the lofty cultural enterprises in Boston — not to mention the activities in Cambridge at the Harvard of Charles W. Eliot — one found in these years the influences of the many immigrants who were pouring into the city. The ambience of Boston was showing the change, as facets of all cultures were being added: blintzes and sauerbraten, babushkas and kimonos, bocci and mahjongg, Saint Lucia's Day and Saint Patrick's Day.

To accommodate the burgeoning population, the legislature had decided in 1893 and 1894 to authorize the Boston Transit Company to build a subway system. Work had begun in March of 1895, and the one and two thirds miles of subway had been opened in September of that year. In 1900 an elevated system was added, to extend the existing routes from downtown Boston at Park Street, Scollay Square, and North Station to South and East Boston. On Marlborough Street, residents objected to trolley cars, so the horse-drawn "Little Green Car and its partner, the Blue Back Bay Car, which left Marlborough Street at Dartmouth and proceeded down Boylston to Tremont, hung on until 1902, long after the rest of the West End Street Railway (parent of the MTA) had been electrified." The early trolleys were colorful: Grove Hall cars were green, Dorchester cars were royal purple, Cambridge was crimson, South Boston scarlet, Brookline pale blue, Brighton brown, and Somerville and Charlestown cars a "defiant" maroon. There was, in addition, a one-truck yellow Belt Line car which traversed Charles Street and downtown Boston to Roxbury Crossing, and down Columbus Avenue back to Charles Street.

At about this time, the De Long Company announced:

The cable-cars may lose their grip
The horse-cars sway and bump;
But one there is that never slips,
Its name is on the million lips
That murmur, See That Hump!
The De Long Hook and Eye

In the first decade of the new century, politics underwent many changes. In 1900, Thomas Hart Norton represented the old guard, with his frugal ideas of city management: his sense of thrift led him to oppose excessive spending on parks and other recreational facilities. He even opposed a subway run by city funds (rather than private funds), but this idea soon went under in the tide of change. The Boston Irish were busily climbing the political ladder of power, and they were of a more friendly than frugal turn of mind as they conducted their political lives with verve and panache. Martin Lomasney was typical of the new breed; as ward boss, he would greet immigrants as they entered the city. All was not sweetness and light, however, for strong-arm tactics were often used at the polls, and the political system was dubbed a "blackjack democracy." It was in this arena that North End Johnny Fitz began his rise. Taking advantage of his athletic contacts, and combining them with his natural showmanship, John F. Fitzgerald became Boston's first popular Irish sovereign in 1905.

Two-year mayoral terms were the rule in those days, however, and Fitzgerald was not re-elected until 1909 when a Beacon Street blue blood, James Jackson Storrow, challenged him. Fitzgerald's campaign slogan, "Manhood against Money," was countered by Storrow's coining of the term "Fitzgeraldism" to describe the dubious antics of Johnny Fitz's first administration. When Fitzgerald sang "Sweet Adeline" at a political rally in Faneuil Hall the Saturday night before the election, ladies swooned, and Johnny Fitz was forever dubbed "Honey Fitz."

The controversy of the campaign, the allegations and political games, were evidenced by headlines of the period: FITZGERALD INSISTS STORROW'S ATTACKS ARE GROSSLY UNFAIR and JAMES J. STORROW IS THE CANDIDATE OF THE MERCHANTS OF BOSTON. In fact, accusations reached such a point that Fitzgerald announced approval of a recount:

FITZGERALD AGREES TO A RECOUNT

New Mayor Wants Clean Office Title

Mayor-elect John F. Fitzgerald today in a statement made to the Boston American, declared that he was in favor of a recount of the mayorality vote by which he was selected over James J. Storrow by 1,416 votes.

The next Mayor says that he does not want to go into office with a shadow on his title to the place. A recount will increase his plurality, he says.

He declares he is going to give Boston the best administration the City ever had. He says he was elected because he and his forces outgeneraled the Storrow people.

Mr. Storrow and the Citizen's Municipal League today obtained papers for a recount of the mayorality vote and began their circulation through the various wards of the city. Fifty signatures in each ward are required. The blank papers were obtained by William C. Pree, secretary of the League.

Expects No Trouble

Clad in the conventional black frock coat, striped trousers and a red four-in-hand that may have lent some of the color to his cheeks, John F. Fitzgerald talked with a reporter in the library of his Wilkes Avenue home. Floating through the halls came sounds of preparation for the departure of his daughter Rose for New York, where she is to attend a finishing school.

BOSTON ADVERTISER
January 12, 1910

On Friday, January 21, headlines read: RE-COUNT DONE; RESULT STANDS.

After John Fitzgerald was re-elected mayor, a popular ballad became known in many quarters of the city, and his legend was begun:

Honey Fitz can talk you blind
On any subject you can find.
Fish or fishing, motor boats,
Proper way to open clams,
How to cure existing shams.
State Street, Goo-Goos, aeroplanes,
Malefactors, thieving gains.
Local transportation rate,
How to run the nearby states.
On all these things and many more
Honey Fitz is crammed with lore.

Those notable accomplishments credited to Honey Fitz include the building of the City Hall Annex, the City Point Aquarium, and the Franklin Park Zoo. With proper respect to patriotism and the American ideal, he declared Columbus Day a legal holiday and gave Mother's Day local sanctity. For the final touch, he initiated the custom of having a Christmas tree on the Boston Common, a tradition still enjoyed to this day.

When older Bostonians recall the second decade of this century, they may remember the opening of the Boston Opera House, and subsequent appearances by Mary Garden and Geraldine Farrar. It was this festive occasion perhaps that indicated the great change soon to arrive in fashion. According to the Boston *Herald*'s account of the grand opening, "The women were beautifully gowned and with many jewels, but there were a few exceptions, especially in the orchestra stalls, to the rule of full evening dress." Major changes were slow in coming, but this perhaps marked the beginning.

Since 1860 the skirt had been growing slowly shorter, and at this time colored stockings were now in vogue. The fashion ranged from gray silk with red cloaks to Scotch plaids, and cotton was universally worn. But in 1912, the "jupe culotte" killed the cotton forever, and silk and rayon began to dominate leg fashion. Not until 1924, however, did really short skirts arrive and stockings for bathers depart.

The teens were a cultural montage. Dorothy Dix and Beatrice Fairfax set standards for love and etiquette, managing to avoid the growing controversy of women's suffrage. Newspapers of the time carried the saccharine verse of Ella Wheeler Wilcox, the antics of the Katzenjammer Kids, a column on boxing by John L. Sullivan, and notes on Boston's "250" in society. While some people kept an eye on Jack Johnson and Jim Jeffries, training for the fight of the decade, others were following the activities of Mrs. John C. Fairchild, generally conceded to be the most beautiful of Boston's exclusive coterie of younger society matrons.

Most society woman shunned controversy, but a few seemed to seek it out. Isabella Stewart Gardner ("Mrs. Jack") kept Boston alive with her antics. She drank beer rather than tea, paraded along Tremont Street with her pet lion, Rex, and scandalized Boston with John Singer Sargent's infamous portrait of herself with pearls around the waist of her low-cut gown. She briefly embraced Buddhism, told risqué stories in mixed company, and was probably the first truly liberated "proper Bostonian." Her boundless concern and generosity toward young as well as recognized artists established her as a genuine patroness of the arts. Her famous house at Fenway Court was called by one historian "the Venetian Renaissance . . . reincarnated in twentieth-century Boston."

Another controversial patroness of the arts — and an artist herself — was Amy Lowell. Through her efforts, a myriad of young poets were heard, among them Robert Frost. She effected a resurgence of interest in Edgar Allan Poe, Emily Dickinson, and Walt Whitman. A poet herself, she became the leader of the imagist school, and in 1915 published the first volume of an anthology, *Some Imagist Poets*. Her own verse came hard. As Van Wyck Brooks pointed out, "She toiled over her poems from midnight till dawn, not as one to whom the muses whispered, but as one who had to wrestle with them and force them to their knees in the sweat of her brow." Her spirit was domineering and manlike, and such habits as smoking big black cigars won for her a reputation of an outrageous person who "strode over the hills and broke them." And yet, her ultimate triumph was not as an eccentric personality, but as poet, critic, and biographer. Her two-volume biography of Keats is considered by some to be her finest work.

Just as Amy Lowell, according to her diary, was "ugly, fat, conspicuous, and dull," so Eleonora Sears was attractive, slender, and vivacious. Like both Mrs. Jack and Miss Lowell, she was the subject of much gossip, and she received ample coverage from newspapers. A typical headline in the Boston *Advertiser* read ELEONORA SEARS IN MEN'S POLO COSTUME THAT STARTLED WEST. Miss Sears frequently shocked contemporaries by showing a preference for men's attire, and by rigorously participating in numerous athletic events such as championship tennis, polo, automobile racing, and cross-country hiking. One of her more daring escapades was her participation in the newly popular sport, aeroplane racing. She flew with Claude Grahame-White, an English pilot who, along with Charles Hamilton and Thomas Sopwith, thrilled spectators with amazing feats of courage and skill.

Life in these times was definitely moving faster than twenty years before — not only physically, because of the automobile and aeroplane, but also socially. By this time, the sons and daughters of the Bullyboys had pushed forward to the front ranks of society. If they could not exactly join the Brahmins, they could match them, and match them they did. Perhaps the most indicative event of the time was the coming-out party of Miss Rose Fitzgerald, Honey Fitz's daughter, in 1911. Approximately four hundred guests attended, including the young and then obscure Joseph P. Kennedy and his family. One press report read as follows:

ROSE FITZGERALD
MAKES HER DEBUT TODAY

Mayor Fitzgerald's Eldest Daughter
Makes Bow to Society

On the day of "her coming out" Miss Rose E. Fitzgerald received a pleasant surprise at the hands of her father, Mayor Fitzgerald, and a number of her girlfriends today. Though most of the Fitzgerald home in Dorchester had been decorated before New Year's, the Mayor saved one part of the residence to be decorated today. This was the upper portion, which serves as Miss Rose's own private bower.

A number of Miss Rose's friends who were in on the surprise feature assisted her in attending to the decorations. The room was the center of life when Miss Rose entertained her own circle of girlfriends. The decorations were of rosebuds—roses appropriate for the debutante, and buds for herself and her chums, all of whom are among the prettiest young society folk in Dorchester.

The family was kept busy, particularly Mayor and Mrs. Fitzgerald and Miss Rose, who was assisted by her eighteen-year-old sister, Agnes. Miss Rose received hundreds of messages by telephone and telegraph, some from across the ocean. One that she prized highly came from the Reverend Mother at Blumenthal Academy, Baals, Holland, where she studied when she was abroad.

The following cable from Sir Thomas Lipton is not the least prized:

"I extend my heartiest congratulations to you on the occasion of your coming out. I suppose that in a short time I will be sending congratulations for another occasion of great joy, that of your marriage. Before that occurs I hope that you will pick out a man who is the equal of your father."

Thomas Lipton

Southern smilax and orchids form the chief decorative feature of the reception room and the debutante and her attendants stood in front of a bower of smilax and orchids while receiving. The large hall is adorned with mountain laurel and the other rooms are similarly decorated. The billiard room has been turned into a dining room for the occasion.

Miss Fitzgerald's dress is of white satin with crepe meteor, the skirt being adorned with yellow silk-ribbon with Italian embroidery. Similar is on the bodice and a demi-train completes the skirt.

In the receiving line, together with Mr. and Mrs. Fitzgerald, were several of the debutantes' young friends, including some of the season's prettiest Dorchester buds. Miss Marguerite O'Callaghan, daughter of J. J. O'Callaghan of Upham's Corner, Miss Molly Welch and Miss Mary L. O'Connell were among those who aided Miss Fitzgerald in receiving."

BOSTON ADVERTISER
January 2, 1911

In the summer of this same year, 1911, the Fitzgeralds sailed for Europe. Boston was suffering the worst heat wave in New England history, but this did not deter Honey Fitz: while people were wilting in the streets, he lustily sang his theme song, "Sweet Adeline," from the bridge of the *Franconia*. When the ship neared the Irish coast, he set off rockets and other fireworks until the Irish Coast Guard finally signaled, "Do you need help?"

He needed no help then, but could have used some the next year, when the street railway workers struck. The strike was particularly unfortunate, for thousands were trying to reach newly completed Fenway Park to see the Boston Americans (now the Red Sox) win the World Series of 1912. As if the strike were not trouble enough, Honey Fitz faced another challenge, this one from James Michael Curley, intent on winning the mayor's seat. Mayoral terms were now four years in length; Fitzgerald had been serving his second term since 1910, and he had made a bosses' agreement to leave City Hall at the end of this term. When Curley announced his candidacy, however, the Mayor reconsidered. A great rivalry developed between the two bosses, and William Cardinal O'Connell, previously Bishop of Boston, asked Curley to withdraw from the race in favor of the older man. Curley refused, and Honey Fitz withdrew his candidacy.

So Curley's reign began, and Honey Fitz retired from public office. Curley was mayor sixteen years in all, off and on, a congressman for four terms, and governor of Massachusetts during the Depression years. Vast city construction keynoted Curley's first term: streets were ripped up, transit lines extended, hospitals built, beaches and playgrounds laid out, historical restoration which began with the Paul Revere House was continued, and public services in general were expanded. Yankee taxpayers found the cost of these projects enormous, and Gentleman Jim managed to live extraordinarily well on the mayor's salary of $10,000 a year.

Mayor Curley was serving his first term when the devastating Great Salem Fire of 1914 broke out. It started in the leather district, and fourteen hours later, on Friday, June 26, half the city was homeless and out of work. Damages were estimated at $25 million, with seven dead, fifty injured, and two hundred missing. Governor Walsh, Mayor Curley, and ex-Mayor Fitzgerald sat down with three to four hundred businessmen of Boston, and, within an hour, raised a cash relief fund of $77,400. Among the contributors were Jordan Marsh ($1000), Shreve, Crump, and Low ($1000), and Filene's ($1000). Henry Clay Frick was probably the most generous single contributor, donating a sum of $25,000 to the fund.

The pace of history quickened during Mayor Curley's first term. At home, the age of the automobile was firmly and finally established with the motorization of the fire department. Telephone service improved, and an underground cable was laid between Boston and Washington. Political and social unrest prompted John L. Sullivan to make a number of off-the-cuff remarks: "We needn't go down to Mexico to find people to insult the flag. Look at those I.W.W. fellows." Or: "The country is all right. America is always right and always will be, even if mistakes are made by those in charge of her affairs." And, again: "The young people of today are all right, too. Of course, lots of them are making fools of themselves with the tango, but that will die out." Meanwhile, in a lighter vein, the city was treated in October 1914 to a visit from the former Mrs. Tom Thumb. Now remarried to Count Magri, the Countess attracted much attention and interest, particularly among children.

The assassination of Archduke Francis Ferdinand and his wife on Sunday, June 28, went virtually unnoticed. Later, however, concerned citizens acted. In September, Samuel J. Elder, president of both the Boston Bar Association and the Massachusetts Peace Society, led a crowd of 10,000 in probably the first antiwar demonstration of the century — the Boston American Peace Rally. The major address of the event was given by Mayor Curley, who stated:

It is my opinion that the best and surest way to stop this war is for the American nation—North and South—to place an embargo on food products. No man can be a good soldier with an empty haversack. As Napoleon put it, the "army travels on its belly."

Sooner or later wheat will be more valuable to our friends across the sea than cannon.

If you should ask my advice, it would be that we adopt resolutions today favoring the appointment of a commission to work with President Wilson and Secretary of State Bryant [sic] to bring together the Presidents of the South American republics in an agreement to establish an absolute embargo on every necessity of life while the war continues.

BOSTON ADVERTISER
September 13, 1914

Mr. Elder was called "the Dr. Sunshine of the Day" because he was so sanguine about the coming of peace.

The movement for peace will now become irresistible. The world will soon say "lay down your arms." Armaments must be limited and no longer be a menace to the peace and comfort and progress of the world.

The peace movement occurred simultaneously with another equally important cause — that of women's suffrage. Mrs. Maude Wood Park was present at Mr. Elder's meeting, representing the Equal Suffrage Association. She stated that "every soldier who was ever brought into the world came at the risk of some woman's life. Every soldier who today lies dead upon the battlefield of Europe is some mother's son."

The suffragettes' cause gained considerable strength during the early teens. By 1914, they had already won the vote in ten states, and Champ Clark, then Speaker of the House, predicted that they would vote in the national election of 1916 or 1920. They spared no effort to display their cause, as for instance in the greatest suffrage parade in Massachusetts history, held in October 1914:

IMMENSE THRONG ON LINE OF MARCH

The greatest suffrage parade Massachusetts ever saw traversed Boston's streets this afternoon, cheered along its route by a tremendous throng — a throng in which women predominated.

The parade, the ''Victory'' parade of those Massachusetts suffragists who on November 2 expect to win the second step toward enfranchisement, was a splendid spectacle, with floats and placards and marching men and women, in costume and in ''mufti.'' Thirty bands participated.

Along toward noon the sun burst through the clouds and flooded the city with sunshine. This was taken by the suffragists as a good omen. They said the golden rays painting the city with yellow augured that the yellow banner of suffrage would be triumphant on election day.

At Suffrage headquarters all was bustle this morning, with the workers putting the last touches on parade preparations.

The opening event of the day's observance came at noon, when Margaret Foley read President Lincoln's Gettysburg address from opposite the Emancipation statue in Park square, laying special emphasis on his historic words, ''This is a governement of the people, by the people, for the people.''

Demands A Square Deal

The rally lasted ten minutes, Miss Foley being the only speaker.

''Women are people,'' she said, ''and if we are to have a true democracy such as Abraham Lincoln spoke of, women should be given a say in governmental affairs.''

She urged the men to give the women a square deal on November 2.

Her address was heard by more than 500 people, mostly men. The colors of suffrage predominated, although a few women and men wearing the ''Anti'' colors were seen in the crowd. The speaker was vigorously cheered at the opening of her speech and at its conclusion when she sped away in an automobile.

Principal among the features of the parade was Miss Alice Stone Blackwell, president of the Massachusetts Association, and the daughter of Lucy Stone, the Bay State's first prominent suffragist.

Helen Keller, the famous blind girl, accompanied by her secretary, was another prominent figure. Miss Keller's part of the program was to send from her carriage to the Governor and to the Mayor her message of thanks for their support.

Miss Virginia Tanner, garbed as ''Victory,'' appeared on a float. No person who saw the last suffrage parade could forget Miss Tanner in her white satin robes and the royal purple wings.

Newspaper Women in Line

Jane Pride's group of newspaper women, the Harvard delegations, undergraduates and faculty members, the cavalry section, the college women's groups, the suffrage spellbinders' division, and the division herald were all notable features.

Many houses along the route of the parade were decorated with the suffrage colors and with red, white, and blue bunting. ''Votes for Women'' badges, yellow roses, daffodils, chrysanthemums and suffrage streamers with yellow predominating.

And of course the antis did their best to offset the yellow. Thousands of red roses, the badge of the anti, were sold in the city. They, too, had their decorations along the route of the parade to taunt the marchers.

BOSTON ADVERTISER
October 16, 1914

Meanwhile life went on as usual, and, with the help of a young pitcher named Babe Ruth, the Boston Red Sox won the World Series in both 1915 and 1916. Braves Field was dedicated in 1917.

In 1919 there occurred an event which shook Boston and brought nationwide attention. When Boston police were forbidden to affiliate with the American Federation of Labor, they went on strike for two days, leaving the Boston population of more than 700,000 people without protection. Mobs ruled the streets, while prominent citizens were appointed special policemen.

The police had legitimate grievances: their minimum pay was $1100 a year, less than half of what many war workers earned. In addition, the two-platoon system forced them to work on twelve-hour shifts. Unionization seemed the most promising way to alleviate these problems.

The authorities saw things differently. All striking members of the force were discharged. Calvin Coolidge, then governor of Massachusetts, called upon the state National Guard to restore order — a move which brought him national recognition.

While Boston felt the impact of both the police strike and the suffragist movement, she was relatively untouched by the war raging in Europe. Reaction would come later, with a major influx of Italian, Irish, and other immigrants to the city. Boston citizens were, however, caught up in the fervor and spirit of wartime preparedness. Rallies were held on the Common, and people became more frugal in the spirit of the war effort. Anti-German feelings and a surge of patriotism began to override traditional Brahmin isolationism. Nevertheless, the grim reality of death and loss tempered wartime enthusiasms: "Over There" soon gave way to "I Didn't Raise My Boy to be a Soldier," a sentiment felt both on Beacon Hill and in the poorer suburban communities.

The attitude of upper-class Bostonians toward the war was later captured by John P. Marquand, in his well-known satire *The Late George Apley* (1937). Though George Apley believed himself a liberal man, he unconsciously mirrored the values of his own class. He was infatuated by a South End Irish girl, Mary Monahan, but married a girl of more acceptable appearances. He believed himself a liberal for considering *Lady Chatterley's Lover* a work of art. "This country is riddled with German spies," he said, "and the brains of the system are located beneath the very shadow of the Capitol Dome in Washington." He felt that all Germans in Boston should be watched, adding, "I believe it is absolutely true, as it is rumored, that concrete emplacements are being built on the hills around Boston for heavy guns and that there are a number of wirelesses along the coast which signal the submarines." Apley's traditional suspicion of the Irish and other Roman Catholics fed the fires of his anti-German feelings. Believing the Church to be sympathetic to the German cause, he noted that several religious institutions had been buying land for schools and orphan asylums, and that the sites were noticeably on "a piece of rising ground, commanding a view of the country for miles around."

During the 1920s, Boston — with the rest of the nation—experienced a "return to normalcy." It was a time of prosperity and stability, particularly for the Brahmins. Though Boston was increasingly a city of contrasts and contradictions, the Boston Brahmins remained supreme, carrying on their traditional way of life. The political structure, as we have seen, had been turned over to the Irish when the first Irish mayor was elected in the 1890s; nevertheless, other businesses and professions — the law, banking, industry, and even the presidency of Harvard — were dominated by the leading Brahmin families. Their social life proceeded along certain set paths: there were the Somerst Club, the Vincent Club, sewing circles for women, Trinity Church on Sunday morning. The Boston Symphony and the Athenaeum were popular, as were small dinner parties in Back Bay or on Beacon Hill. It was a time of propriety and acceptability. Also hypocrisy: business mistakes and even illegal actions were overlooked, though similar mistakes by the rising Irish upper classes received full exposure. But for the most part, the values of the Brahmins, if unimaginative, were genuine and safe. Much of the old that was good was well preserved.

If there was little cultural progress or social reform in the 1920s, there were nevertheless many civic improvements. A high-pressure water system for fire extinguishing, using powerful pumping stations instead of portable engines, was put into use. Three new social services were established: the Community Service of Boston, the Boston Council for Social Agencies, and the Boston Health League. For all their narrowness, the best Bostonians had a distinct sense of public duty. They may have turned their backs upon the flood of Irish and Italian immigrants, but they took active part in the preservation of the public safety and cultural amenities.

While proper Bostonians were leading quiet and unobtrusive lives, one man was doing all he could to stay in the limelight. Running for a second term as mayor, James Michael Curley waged a campaign in 1921 that was called "the most vicious and vituperative in Boston's history." Gentlemen Jim fought alone. He waged a powerful smear campaign on his opponent, John H. Murphy, a respected Catholic lawyer. Women by this time had the vote, and were voting for the first time in a Boston election; it was generally believed that Mary Curley's "Personal Appeal to Women Voters," an open letter printed and circulated before the election, turned the opposing tide.

Curley's second term saw an expansion of Boston's commerce and industry. The Bureau of Commerce and Industry and the Municipal Employment Bureau were established. Within two months after the Employment Bureau's creation, the number of unemployed in the city was reduced from about 75,000 to 45,000. At the same time a retirement act providing for employees of the City of Boston was approved.

In 1921 the Republican State Legislature passed a law that no mayor of Boston might succeed himself. Undaunted, in 1924, Mayor Curley ran as the Democratic candidate for governor against Alvan T. Fuller, but lost in a Republican year.

Malcolm E. Nichols was elected mayor in 1925, and it was his administration that in 1927 weathered the review of the controversial case of Nicola Sacco and Bartolomeo Vanzetti. These two Italian anarchists, tried in an atmosphere of suspicion and bigotry, in 1921 had been convicted on circumstantial evidence of a crime they most likely did not commit — a payroll robbery and a double murder. The committee appointed to review the case, headed by President Lowell of Harvard, upheld the original verdict and Sacco and Vanzetti were executed on August 22, 1927. Demonstrations of sympathy for the accused men were staged throughout the country, and a large funeral procession passed through Boston to Forest Hills.

Bostonians have always considered themselves cultured and well informed, and there is much truth in their assumptions. During the 1920s several daily and evening newspapers were active, bringing the news to thousands of Bostonians. One of the papers, the *Traveler*, celebrated its hundredth anniversary on July 5, 1922. Beacon Hill readers still preferred the Boston *Evening Transcript*, a fact documented in T. S. Eliot's poem "The *Boston Evening Transcript*." In literary matters, however, Bostonians were considerably less enlightened. A major controversy broke out in 1928 over censorship policy. Theodore Dreiser's *An American Tragedy*, Upton Sinclair's *Oil*, and one issue of *The American Mercury* were among the publications excluded from Boston bookshelves and bookstores. In 1929 Eugene O'Neill's play *Strange Interlude* was withdrawn from production in Boston after a conference with city authorities, and it was subsequently produced in Quincy.

The teens and roaring twenties in Boston had been lively, full of graft and corruption, spirited political battles, improvements and advances of various kinds. As if to cap the clamor, two devastating events occurred in 1929. One was an earthquake which shook New England and eastern Canada on November 18. The upper floors of the Customs House swayed while pendulum clocks stopped in the State House. The other event — the stock market crash of October—had a far more devastating effect on the city, though that effect did not make itself felt immediately.

By 1930, Boston was still a relatively prosperous U.S. city, ranking eighth in population. Most of her citizens were Irish, reaching in some families into the fourth generation. The country was a century and a half old; Boston was twice that age. And in a regeneration of youth — or in a degeneration of old age — Boston had elected James Michael Curley mayor for the third nonconsecutive term.

The city that celebrated its two hundredth anniversary was a patchwork quilt of the old and the new. Old institutions continued to endure: the Boston Symphony Orchestra celebrated its fiftieth anniversary in 1930, and the political machinery forged in the later years of the nineteenth century was likewise half a century old. Old notions of propriety and restraint continued to be influential: John M. Casey, the Boston censor, still guarded public morality from the "dangers" of dubious books and plays. Brahmin Abbott Lawrence Lowell continued in office as president of Harvard until 1933.

No man more clearly epitomized the tenor of Boston life in these days than Mayor Curley, now in his third term. It was his spirit that made it possible for Boston to weather the Depression, now making its effects visible. Curley worked against the downward tide of the Depression, in particular by means of building programs. Finding Boston still a city of cow paths, narrow winding streets, and back alleys, he announced on his inauguration day a fifty-year building program. Results were good: the Callahan Tunnel, the Kenmore Square MTA Station, and the MTA network connecting Boston to Logan Airport were completed during his years in office. Partly to combat the Depression, and partly to serve the Boston Irish, Curley planned beaches, playgrounds, and parks. New buildings appeared; streets were extensively repaved. The face of the city was changing.

Along with construction, Curley's strong personality inspired something else: a legend. One story about Curley concerns Boston's plans for honoring its great men who had died in the First World War. On this occasion Mayor Curley instructed his aide to honor as well the Mayor's long-time assistant and alter ego, Standish Willcox, by placing (most unobtrusively) a bottle of sauterne on his grave. One week later, on his way home from City Hall, the Mayor instructed his chauffeur to stop at Standish's grave and (equally unobtrusively) retrieve the wine. "He would have wanted it that way," explained James Michael.

Building projects cost money. Taxpayers felt the pinch, and the city debt swelled. It was a large debt fed by years of graft and neglect. Curley contributed to the problem in various ways; indeed, the Finance Committee of Boston had been investigating his affairs for almost twenty years. When Curley stepped down in 1934 and Frederick W. Mansfield took over as mayor, investigations were stepped up. Mansfield dedicated himself to Curley's annihilation, and he succeeded, at least temporarily, in this cause. By 1936, public suspicion of Curley was such that he was forced out of the political scene for six years.

Curley's downfall was also caused by another curious phenomenon. In the late 1930s the Boston Irish and the Boston Brahmins were beginning to discover each other. For years the Brahmins had controlled the financial structure of the city, while the Irish had controlled the vote. Now, during the Depression, even the Brahmins were feeling the strain. An attitude of lofty hauteur was no longer possible. Taking a good look at the Irish, after four generations of inattention, the Brahmins found that in many

cases the Irish had become more Brahmin in mind and manner than the Brahmins themselves. There was no reason why the two groups should not combine strength and work together in financial and political circles. The coalition led to Curley's fall. Always hated by the Brahmins, no longer needed by the Bullyboys, the charismatic figure who had dominated Boston for over a quarter of a century was eased out.

Rejected by the people he had worked for most, burdened with the ever-increasing files from the Finance Committee's investigation, Curley's career seemed at an end. He was beaten for U.S. senator in 1936 by Henry Cabot Lodge, Jr., and for mayor in 1937 by his own protégé, Maurice J. Tobin. Never one to admit defeat, however, he continued the political game. In 1938 he lost out for governor to Leverett Saltonstall, and, in 1940, to Tobin again for mayor. (The law conveniently had been changed so that Tobin could succeed himself as mayor and thus prevent Curley's re-election.)

During the 1940s the Boston economy experienced two radical shifts. At first, in the period immediately following Pearl Harbor, the city began slowly to prosper. Navy yards, shipyards, and manufacturing companies operated on government contracts. Employment rose. Sailors came into town on weekends, and the nightclub business flourished. Thus Boston—which had never felt the full weight of the Depression and therefore had never really acknowledged it — was free of all economic pressures. Spirits were high, in the way they often are when an urgent common cause gives people a strong boost to morale. With the end of the war, however, the surge of prosperity began to subside. As war contracts were canceled, workers in such industries as textiles and leather goods were laid off by the thousands. The Foye shipyard closed down. Boston took on the aura of a ghost town. Twenty-two of the twenty-six night-clubs in the city closed their doors forever. Parks, roads, beaches, and streets suffered from neglect. Prices soared, food was short, the housing situation was critical.

At this point, the people remembered Curley. The Finance Committee that had been investigating Curley had ordered him to turn over $42,000 to the city in repayment for "misdirected funds." Curley had been broken and depressed by his defeat. His plight had aroused sufficient sympathy to get him elected to Congress, and by 1946 the people were ready to elect him mayor once again. He had pulled them through one Depression, and people felt that he could do so again. Furthermore, while Curley's own people could criticize him, they felt it unfair for anyone else to attack the "native son." By and large Boston's voters remained true to him — in spite of the fact that he was sentenced to prison, and began in June of 1947 to serve that sentence in Danbury Prison. Indeed, it seemed that despite Curley's duels with both Brahmins and Bullyboys, Bostonians felt it unfair to remove him from office while he was in jail. When released five months later, around Thanksgiving Day, he found himself still in office. There ensued a battle to throw him out again, but Curley prevailed. At seventy-four, he was a vigorous mayor: he still put in ten to fourteen hours a day at City Hall, and he was contemplating a building program that would lead to the construction of Storrow Drive. The prison cloud evaporated.

Television came to Boston. In an early interview on the screen, Curley was asked, "How long do you expect to live, Mr. Mayor?"

"I expect to live to be one hundred and twenty-five years old, and I also expect to be mayor of Boston all that time."

This characteristic remark sums up all that Curley was, through a long life of energetic political fighting. Unique in Boston's history, Curley's style and personality sparked people's imaginations, and among these was Edwin O'Connor, who re-created the real man in the figure of Frank Skeffington in *The Last Hurrah*. O'Connor, a devout Catholic, viewed the passing of the Irish politician as the end of a colorful era. He saw the absorption of the Irish-American community as the tragic consequence of this loss of power, and considered absorption an end of ethnic cultural identity. But Irish integration into American society was inevitable, just as it had been for other immigrants before them.

The plot of *The Last Hurrah* revolves around Skeffington's last campaign for re-election as mayor at the age of seventy-two. O'Connor gives a full-length portrait of Skeffington as a corrupt and powerful, but understanding and generous, head of a political machine. He covers a wide social spectrum, including conflicts between the Irish and the Yankees, the old and the young, the lay and the clerical leaders, and, finally, between the old locally based politicians and the new federally oriented system. He explains Skeffington's defeat not as the defeat of an individual party boss, but rather as the end of a generation of party bosses. The death of the Irish politician simply illustrates the destruction of the personal basis of power throughout the country. The death of Skeffington at the end of this novel was necessary, for he, like Curley, had the audacity, imagination, and skill to stand up to society. Unfortunately, he was doomed to failure because the basis of his support, the Irish-American community, deserted him. "He has played the old game too long, and the Irish have changed too much.'' The personal magnetism and mastery of individual and crowd psychology died with Skeffington. His loyal followers were left without an object of devotion and his enemies without an object of disdain. His exit left them enveloped in a cloud of moral emptiness and political bathos.

Evidently there was more of a parallel to Curley than he would have liked to admit, for in August of 1958 he went to court seeking to ban the motion picture version of the novel, in which the late Spencer Tracy played the lead. Curley was unsuccessful and the case was settled out of court. His image faded from the screen, his influence moved slowly into the realm of the forgotten, to be only nominally remembered. Boston moved, along with a growing and ever-prospering postwar America, into a new age —

an age of advanced technology and communications, an age of televisions in every home, of two-car garages and commercial jets to Europe, of lunar exploration, and the atom bomb. Boston, too, moved into the Space Age.

Still around us are reminders of our unknown pasts, the museums and architecture of decades and centuries ago, the art and literature passed down from other times, the monuments raised to those deemed worthy of remembrance. Boston is rich in these aesthetic reminders, and somehow has preserved a certain essence of yesterday, a feeling of past in present. And to the memorabilia of Boston and New England G. Frank Radway added and preserved intact on paper moments in time that would have otherwise been forgotten forever.

THE POLITICAL LIFE

Honey Fitz handing out more than fifteen hundred Christmas baskets at Salvation Army headquarters, People's Palace, Boston, December 24, 1910. Salvation Army Colonel Grifford and Mrs. Fitzgerald are to the left of the mayor

Honey Fitz at the start of the Boston Marathon.
Ashland, Massachusetts, April 1911

Mayor Fitzgerald and family on board the *Franconia* just prior to their departure for Europe. Daughter Agnes (*left*), Mrs. Fitzgerald and daughter Rose (*right*). Boston, June 27, 1911

Vote counting at the Fitzgerald-Storrow recount. Final results confirmed Fitzgerald's re-election as mayor. Faneuil Hall, Boston, January 1910

"Candidate of the merchants," James J. Storrow. Boston, December 1915

(*Left to right*) Joseph W. Powell, vice president of the Bethlehem Shipbuilding Corporation; Charles M. Schwab, director general of the Emergency Fleet Corporation; and a young, then unknown Boston businessman named Joseph P. Kennedy. Boston, circa 1915

President Taft addressing a crowd at the Cotton Centennial Carnival
on President's Day. Fall River, Massachusetts, June 1911

Derby-hatted throng at a Boston labor demonstration

Great crowds demonstrating outside Faneuil Hall against the imprisonment of Samuel Gompers and Morrison I. Swift. March 1909

Labor confrontation in Boston at the State House. (*Left to right*) Sergeant at Arms Remmington; Police Sergeant M. J. Crowley; and Morrison I. Swift, leader of the unemployed. March 1909

Right Unidentified police official with labor leader Samuel Gompers, following his arrest for his part in 1909 labor agitations. Boston, March 1909

Mrs. Philip Snowden, English suffragette leader. Boston, 1909

President Taft and his daughter, Helen, on the steps of their new summer house in Beverly Farms, Massachusetts. July 1, 1911

(*Left to right*) Helen Keller, her secretary, Pauline Thompson, and her teacher, Mrs. J. A. Macy. Photograph taken in Boston, October 16, 1914, when Miss Keller took part in Boston's suffragette parade of over ten thousand women

Right Young woman voting in Boston. November 1921

Coolidge family portrait at his inauguration as the forty-eighth governor of Massachusetts. (*Left to right*) Calvin Coolidge, Jr., Mrs. Coolidge, Governor Coolidge, and John Coolidge. State House, Boston, January 2, 1919

Mayor and Mrs. James Michael Curley. Boston, 1925

(*Left to right*) Boston Mayor James Michael Curley and ex-Mayor Thomas Norton Hart. City Hall, February 5, 1923

CELEBRITIES & VISITORS

Financier J. Pierpont Morgan, Jr. (*left*), Junius Spencer Morgan, and the former's fiancée, Miss Louise Converse. Boston, circa 1920

Famous wedding day photograph of actress Ethel Barrymore and Russell Griswold Colt, son of
Colonel Samuel Pomeroy Colt, president of the U.S. Rubber Company and the Industrial Trust
Company of Providence, Rhode Island. Fairchild Place, Dedham, Massachusetts, March 14, 1909

Scottish entertainer Sir Harry Lauder. Boston, November 1909

Evelyn Nesbit Thaw, later known as "The Girl on the Golden Swing," wife of Harry K. Thaw, who murdered noted architect Stanford White in a fit of jealousy. Boston, October 20, 1913

Metropolitan Opera favorite Geraldine Farrar in Boston
for her performance of Puccini's *Tosca*, circa 1914

Actress Pauline Frederick. Boston, 1914

(*Left to right*) Count and Countess Magri, the former Mrs. Tom Thumb (aged 73), and the Count's brother, Baron Magri, in Boston for their appearance in *Two Strings to Her Bow* and *The Enchanted Statue.* October 1914

Last known photograph taken of Theodore Roosevelt, shown here with daughter-in-law Grace and newest grandson Archibald Bulloch Roosevelt, Jr. Lockwood, Bay State Road, Boston. March 29, 1918

Electrical engineer Dr. Charles P. Steinmetz.
Boston, circa 1920

President and Mrs. Warren G. Harding at the Pilgrim Tercentenary celebration at Holmes Field, Plymouth, Massachusetts. August 1, 1921

Mrs. Harding receiving a bouquet of flowers and a scroll from Girl Scout leader Mrs. James J. Storrow at the Pilgrim Tercentenary celebration. Plymouth, Massachusetts, August 1, 1921

(*Left to right*) French occultist and apostle of autosuggestion Émile Coué, pictured with George B. Hunt of Boston. Coué is noted for his incantation ''Day by day, in every way, I am getting better and better.'' Back Bay Station, Boston, January 30, 1922

Henry Ford. Boston, circa 1925

Dr. Albert Einstein. Boston, circa 1934

United States golf champion Francis D. Ouimet as an army lieutenant with his bride, the former Stella M. Sullivan of Brighton, Massachusetts. September 11, 1918

THE BRAHMIN ACCENT

Dr. Edward Everett Hale, chaplain of the U.S. Senate, addressing a Sunday meeting in Roxbury, Massachusetts. July 12, 1908

Dr. Hale. Boston, June 28, 1908

Author and editor William Dean Howells. Boston, July 25, 1911

"Unconventional Photo of Leading Society Women." Mrs. Reginald C. Vanderbilt (*left*) and Miss Eleonora Sears at Brockton Fair, Brockton, Massachusetts. October 5, 1910

Alfred G. Vanderbilt at the Brockton Fair, October 5, 1910. He was to lose his life on the *Lusitania* on May 7, 1915.

Vincent Astor, son and heir to the fortune of John Jacob Astor, as a freshman at Harvard. Photograph taken during a heavy rainstorm. Cambridge, Massachusetts, October 4, 1911

The Battle of Roses at Wellesley College. Wellesley, Massachusetts, May 8, 1916

Two Brahmin weddings

69

Mrs. H. C. Clark (*left*) and Dorothy Jordan at Beverly Farms, Massachusetts, July 15, 1915

Helen Frick (*left*), daughter of Henry Clay Frick, and Rosamond Bradley at Saint John's Episcopal Church fair. Beverly Farms, Massachusetts, July 15, 1915

Honey Fitz and Sir Thomas Lipton. Boston, 1923

CITY SCENES & FACES

Yankee heritage. Boston, 1900

Damming up the Charles River. Boston, 1908

New fire-fighting equipment introduced by Mayor Curley, marking the end of the horse-drawn engines.
Boston, 1914

All they could save

Three photographs taken just after the Great Salem Fire, June 1914

Automobile and ruins

Elis Melanson managed to save a pet cat

Colonel George B. Billings, Immigration Commissioner for the Port of Boston.
December 1910

Two young immigrants arriving from Italy. Boston, March 1911

Boston faces, circa 1910

84

Iroquois chief. Boston, 1910

Band of full-blooded Iroquois Indians in front of the Craigie-Longfellow House.
Cambridge, Massachusetts, 1910

Buffalo Bill's Wild West Show arriving in Boston. June 1916

Dancing gypsies. Boston, circa 1910

Wreckage of L train which hurtled into the air at the Dudley Street terminal. One fatality; damage estimated at $50,000. Boston, August 4, 1910

Trolley accident on the Broadway Bridge. South Boston, June 12, 1912

Horse thief Mrs. Mabel A. L. Robinson being taken to court by Officer P. Leonard of Mansfield, Massachusetts. Attleboro, Massachusetts, August 4, 1914

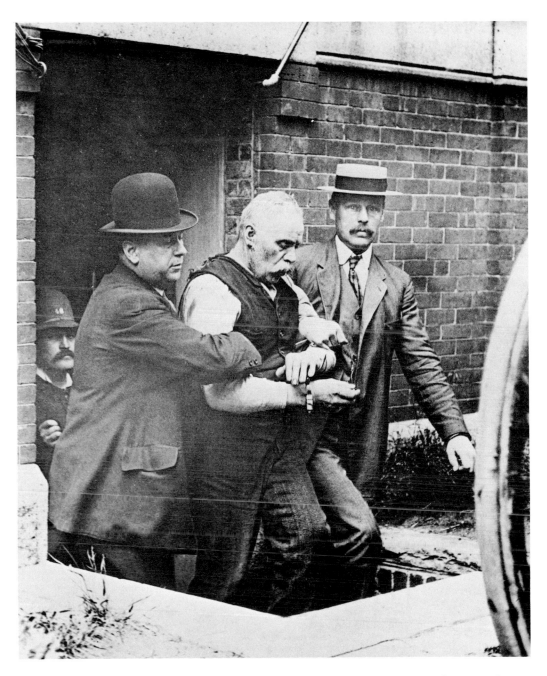

John Murphy, the "Maniac Slayer" of Somerville, Massachusetts, who went insane at the North Packing and Provisions Company on June 5, 1909, killing five men with a knife before he was overpowered. Murphy is here being transferred from Somerville Jail to East Cambridge. June 7, 1909.

Looking south on Summer Street. Boston, January 1910

Left Helen von Moty, former countess and Follies beauty, whose cheek was slashed with
a razor by a former lover. Boston, December 18, 1923

Making a movie. Boston, September 1909

Fourth of July crowd on boardwalk. Revere Beach, Massachusetts, 1914

Unusual accident between automobile and trolley when a Mr. Ray, owner and driver of the auto, "became confused." Photograph taken in front of City Hall, Cambridge, Massachusetts. July 3, 1911

Elvira Dolores "Dolly" Guidone, a sixteen-year-old Hartford, Connecticut, girl who was put on a train bound for New York, but disappeared, and was found a few days later at South Station. Photograph shows her with matron at police headquarters, awaiting the arrival of her parents. August 13, 1915

Tremont Street shopper takes trip into the air — Julia F. Burleigh of Cambridge, Massachusetts, sitting atop ash hoist in front of R. H. Stearns department store, Boston, December 16, 1910. Mrs. Burleigh was walking along Tremont Street when, without warning, the ash hoist rose just as she was walking across it, carrying her fifteen feet into the air. It was quickly lowered and the terrified woman removed.

Semaphore, the forerunner of the stoplight, regulating traffic at the corner of Tremont and Winter streets. Boston, January 24, 1916

Delores Galli (*center*) and members of a Boston ballet company. Boston, November 7, 1911

A cow enters Boston Workhouse Parade. Boston, May 30, 1910

An eleven-hundred-pound turtle, the largest ever brought to T Wharf. Boston, June 26, 1912

Fire in the Vera Chemical Works at Stoneham, Massachusetts. September 22, 1910

John L. Sullivan and his new bride, the former Kate Harkins, sailing for Europe on a Cunard liner. February 8, 1910

John L. Sullivan at home in his arbor. Boston, circa 1914

The Old Manse at Concord, Massachusetts, 1914. Shown here before restoration, the house is weatherbeaten but impressive, surrounded by venerable trees and filled with memories of Emerson and Hawthorne.

On April 19, 1775, Emerson's grandfather, a clergyman, stood at a window of the Old Manse and watched his parishioners gather on the far side of the Concord River to stop the advance of a line of British troops. He saw the first shots fired and smelled the smoke from the burnt powder

The Monroe Tavern, Lexington, Massachusetts, 1914. Built in 1695, it was later used by Lord Percy as headquarters and hospital in 1775, and by George Washington as headquarters during his last New England tour in 1789

The Paul Revere House, Numbers 19 to 21 North Square, before restoration. Boston, 1907

The Paul Revere House after restoration by the Paul Revere Memorial Association, 131 years after his famous ride. Boston, 1909

Archbishop O'Connell (*left*) and Reverend James H. O'Neill, pastor of Sacred Heart Church, East Boston. June 30, 1911

POPULAR PASTIMES & AMUSEMENTS

"Fight fiercely, Harvard." Cambridge, Massachusetts, circa 1910

Miss Madeline Burlow posing in a daring swimming costume for
the period. Revere Beach, Massachusetts, 1910

Contestants lined up for the biggest swimming match ever held in Boston. On August 23, 1914, 121 women participated in a 1.5-mile race down the Charles River. Only 45 women finished. Marion Gibson, who swam the then unpolluted Charles in just over 58 minutes, won the race.

World champion Boston Red Sox pitching staff. (*Left to right*) Sad Sam Jones, Carl Mays, Babe Ruth, and an unidentified fourth player at opening of the 1915 World Series. Fenway Park, September 9, 1915

Boston Red Sox manager Bill Carrigan shows the winning team's share of the 1915 World Series, a check in the amount of $86,939.73, each player receiving $3951.80. Boston, October 14, 1915

Manager Ed Barrows and Pitcher Sad Sam Jones of the Red Sox just before the fourth game of the 1918 World Series between the Boston Red Sox and the Chicago Cubs. Boston, September 9, 1918

Boxing promoter Tex Rickard. Boston, 1909

Walter J. "Rabbit" Maranville of the Boston Braves as sportswriter for the
Boston American. Boston, October 1, 1915

Claude Grahame-White in his biplane with passenger A. A. Merrill. Harvard Aviation Field, September 24, 1910

Eugene Ely in a Curtiss biplane ready for a flight. Harvard Boston Aero Meet, September 2, 1911

(*Left to right*) Clarence N. Barron of the reception committee and Miss Grahame-White, sister of Claude Grahame-White, with aviators Thomas Sopwith and Claude Grahame-White, watching a flight. Harvard Boston Aero Meet, September 2, 1911

Finish of the four-cylinder, thirty-horsepower Maxwell car nonstop engine run of 10,000 miles that started March 18, 1909 and ended April 12, 1909, at Copley Square, Boston.

Up the State House steps. Early automobile publicity-stunt photograph shows actor Harold Duquesne from the Keith Vaudeville circuit driving miniature racing car up the steps of the State House. Boston, October 22, 1918

Baseball great Tris Speaker in publicity photograph as a soldier. Boston, 1915

First Corps cadets marching through Park Square just before a week of camping and basic preparation prior to their departure for Europe. Boston, July 10, 1915

Over 1000 members of the Harvard Student Regiment marching down Columbus Avenue during Boston's "preparedness" parade. May 27, 1916

Right Vivian Segal, leading lady of the *Oh, Lady, Lady* company, costumed in the national colors as she sang "The Star-spangled Banner" at the Daisy Day Drive on the Boston Common for the 101st Regiment. September 7, 1918

Selected Readings

Back Bay Boston: The City as a Work of Art. Boston: Museum of Fine Arts, 1969.

Boston Society of Architects. *Boston Architecture.* Cambridge: Massachusetts Institute of Technology Press, 1970.

Bowen's Picture of Boston, or the Citizen's and Stranger's Guide. Boston: Otis, Broaders and Company, 1838.

Brooks, Van Wyck. *New England: Indian Summer.* New York: E. P. Dutton and Company, 1940.

Cameron, Gail. *Rose: A Biography of Rose Fitzgerald Kennedy.* New York: G. P. Putnam's Sons, 1971.

Carter, Morris. *Isabella Stewart Gardner and Fenway Court.* Boston: Houghton Mifflin Company, 1940.

Copley Square. Boston: State Street Trust Company, 1941.

Crawford, Mary Caroline. *Romantic Days in Old Boston.* Boston: Little, Brown and Company, 1910.

Dickens, Charles. *American Notes for General Circulation.* New York, 1847.

Drake, Samuel Adams. *Old Landmarks of Boston.* Boston: James R. Osgood and Company, 1875.

Emerson, Edward Waldo. *The Early Years of the Saturday Club.* Boston: Houghton Mifflin Company, 1918.

Holmes, Oliver Wendell. *The Autocrat of the Breakfast Table.* Boston: James R. Osgood and Company, 1872.

———. *Over the Teacups.* Boston: Houghton Mifflin Company, 1891.

Howe, M. A. de Wolfe. *Boston, the Place and the People.* New York: Macmillan Company, 1903.

Howells, William Dean. *Suburban Sketches.* Boston: James R. Osgood and Company, 1872.

———. *Literary Friends and Acquaintances.* New York: Harper and Brothers, 1901.

———. *The Rise of Silas Lapham.* New York: Random House, Modern Library, 1951.

Lawrence, Robert Means. *Old Park Street and Its Vicinity.* Cambridge: Houghton Mifflin Company, Riverside Press, 1922.

Linscott, Robert N., ed. *State of Mind: A Boston Reader.* New York: Farrar, Straus and Company, 1948.

McCord, David. *About Boston: Sight, Sound, Flavor and Inflection.* Boston: Little, Brown and Company, 1948.

Marquand, John P. *The Late George Apley.* Boston: Little, Brown and Company, 1937.

Morison, Samuel Eliot. *One Boy's Boston, 1887–1901.* Boston: Houghton Mifflin Company, 1962.

O'Connor, Edwin. *The Last Hurrah.* Boston: Little, Brown and Company, 1956.

Payne, Edward, F. *Dickens' Days in Boston.* Cambridge: Houghton Mifflin Company, Riverside Press, 1927.

Ross, Marjorie Drake. *The Book of Boston: The Victorian Period.* New York: Hastings House Publishers, 1964.

Thwing, Annie Haven. *The Crooked and Narrow Streets of the Town of Boston, 1630–1822.* Boston: Marshall Jones Company, 1920.

Whitehill, Walter Muir. *Boston: A Topographical History.* 2d rev. ed., Cambridge: Harvard University Press, Belknap Press, 1968.

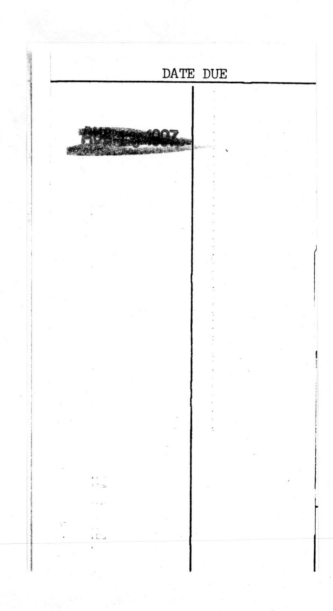

DATE DUE